IMPOSSIBLE

SAM MILLER

LIFE LESSONS ON THRIVING WITH A DISABILITY

Special discounts are available on quantity purchases by corporations, associations, and others. Orders by US trade bookstores and wholesalers—for details, contact the author via the website above.

This publication is intended to provide helpful and informative material on the subjects addressed. Readers should consult their personal health professionals before adopting any of the suggestions in this book or drawing inferences from it. The authors and publisher expressly disclaim responsibility for any adverse effects arising from the use or application of the information contained in this book. Sam is not a medical doctor, or licensed medical or health care professional. He is an author and speaker. Nothing in this book should be seen as individual medical advice.

Cover and interior design by Chelsea Phillips
Headshot photo by JD Hudson

ISBN: 978-1-7332548-7-8

DEDICATION

To my beautiful and talented wife, Kayla. Thank
you for all your love. You constantly remind me
that the impossible is possible.

ENDORSEMENTS

"I contracted Sam as an instructor for our program centered around transitioning students into the community. I observed Sam inspiring my students and building rapport with them during his instruction. Multiple students reported significant gains in confidence, creativity and employment. I am excited to see the impact of his book!"

GREG CASSIDY
Chief Operating Officer
Tazewell County Resource Centers

"I have known Sam Miller for more than twenty years. He is a principled and sincere person whose grit and sense of purpose have helped him surmount many challenges. His story, and the thoughts that accompany it, are inspiring."

BOB COSTAS
American Sportscaster

"Sam spoke to my group. One hundred percent said they were inspired by being challenged to live out their dreams and to share them with others also!"

JERRY FIELDS
Co-Founder, Ability Project

"I've known Sam for close to 20 years, beginning when I was his teacher and speech team coach in high school. Over the years, I've watched Sam grow from a timid, yet eager and caring young man to a man who embodies his message of overcoming obstacles and breaking down barriers in a powerful way that any audience can benefit from."

SUSIE KNOBLAUCH
Assistant Executive Director
Illinois High School Association

"Sam Miller is an incredible resource for youth with disabilities and their families, whose research and wisdom are both empathetic and instructive. My work in this space is smarter and better because of Sam. I'm personally smarter and better because of him too."

WILL LEITCH
Author of *How Lucky*

"I'm inspired to watch Sam be a powerful man who refuses to bow at adversity. He carries an infectious faith that everyone can be powerful and impact the world around them. You will be ignited in your hope for a better tomorrow when you finish what he's written in these pages. I am excited with you for what tomorrow has in store for you!"

DANNY SILK
President of Loving on Purpose
Author of Keep Your Love On and Unpunishable

CONTENTS

PART NINE

PART TEN

ACKNOWLEDGMENTS

For someone who thinks you can learn from everybody you meet, it was hard for me to put together a list of acknowledgments. The list could be miles long! Ultimately, I decided to acknowledge and thank those who were directly involved in making this book happen. If I left you out, I'm so sorry!

Molly Anderson
Ben Armstrong
Heather Armstrong
Kira Armstrong
Madison Armstrong
Matt Bain
Lindsey Brewer
Jeremy Butrous
Greg Cassidy
Josh Cawley
Bob Costas
Eric Eidson
Tom Harpham
Susie Knoblauch
Paul Krismanits
Summer Krismanits
Dennis LaRue, Jr.
Rick Larson
Ray Leight

Will Leitch
Christian Lewis
Karen Lewis
Dave Look
Paul Martinelli
Eddy Martinez
Kelli Metzler
Logan Metzler
Richard Mobley
Adam Moser
Annie Mutti
Megan Mutti
Andrew Ngui
Aaron Phillips
Chelsea Phillips
Shirley Pritzker
Jeremiah Psinas
Chris Rothert
Danielle Seybold

Danny Silk
Denise Steffen-Brewer
Andy Thomas
Chris Tracy
Angela Williams

And finally, to my family, I'm more grateful to you than I can put into words.

INTRODUCTION

I'm possible? "What do you mean by 'I'm possible'?" you may be asking. Allow me to introduce myself. I'm Sam Miller, and I'm possible. You are too.

I want to invite you to join me on a dream journey, a journey of going from impossible to possible. In my experience, something is always possible. There is always something we can do to move us toward our dreams and goals. But before we think about doing, it's important to look at who we are.

I have cerebral palsy. Born prematurely with underdeveloped lungs, not enough oxygen reached my brain, which left the lower half of my body and my left side not working normally. The good news is, my condition isn't progressive. The not-so-good news is, without a miracle, I won't get much better.

I've endured five orthopedic surgeries and hours of physical therapy. I've fallen countless times. Still, more hurtful than the physical pain I experienced was the isolation I felt when I was excluded from my peers' activities. It didn't help that for my first few years of school I was bussed fifteen miles away for therapy. Yet, I came to a place where I knew there had to be something good that could come out of pain and suffering. How could my experiences make me better off?

For most of my life, I've felt caught in the middle. Cerebral palsy impacts every day of my life, but I'm definitely on the more mild end of the spectrum. I'm eternally grateful but there are plenty of days when I still find myself striving and full of questions. I think about the sporting events I missed out on, the dances, jobs and other ordinary activities that are easy for others to take for granted. At the same time, I recognize activities like those are what we often live for. There are days when I feel so close, yet so far from "normal." Who came up with the definition of normal, anyway?

But I didn't write this book to talk about myself. I wrote this book because I want to help youth and families affected by disabilities. I want to help you re-define "normal." Who you are and who you are becoming is not about "conforming to a standard; usual; typical," as the definition of normal suggests. If you're like me, you're longing for what's in your heart to become your ever-increasing reality. I want you to know that who you are— your dreams and goals are possible.

I believe that what I've gone through can help you. That's why I chose to share 10 life lessons on thriving with a disability in this book. They are not just nice ideas. They are gold nuggets from my journey, lessons I've stumbled through and fought for in search of a better life. Join me on the journey of going from surviving to thriving.

During a visit to Ford's Theatre in Washington, D.C.
I stuck close to my dad. I had heard that Abraham
Lincoln was killed here, and I didn't want to be next
in line.

PART ONE

CONQUERING FEAR

Has fear held you back from your dreams and goals? Or do you refuse to let fear have the final say? The choice is yours.

Lesson 1

OUT OF MY CONTROL

I've always had quite the imagination. It's part of what has allowed me to dream and do, and help others do the same. Of course, as with most strengths, there is a potential downside. On one side of imagination are the positives of what's possible. On the other side, there are the negatives—like fear.

Fear has tried to get the better of me from as early as I can remember. One of my first conscious fights with fear happened when I was four years old. My parents took me sightseeing in Washington, D.C. When we came to Ford's Theatre, I made sure someone I trusted checked to ensure the coast was clear.

In case you need a refresher, this is the location of Abraham Lincoln's assassination, one of the most well-known deaths in United States history. As the president sat in his box at Ford's Theatre, the actor John Wilkes Booth shot him. Growing up in the Land of Lincoln meant it didn't take long for the tale to make a lasting impression on me. It seemed almost present-day in my young mind.

I insisted, if John Wilkes Booth were still on the prowl, Mom should take the hit and protect my Dad and me. To reassure me, she entered the theater first and did a quick walk-through. Fortunately, there was no sign of the assassin. Sufficiently convinced, I cautiously decided to go in, but I stuck as close as I could to Mom and Dad. When we emerged unscathed, I was elated. I think I even celebrated my survival with ice cream.

You might shake your head or laugh at a story like this, but allow me to explain. I was born with cerebral palsy. I came into the world too early. Instead of being placed in my mother's arms, I was immediately transferred to a neonatal intensive care unit at another hospital. Suddenly, the familiar and comforting sound of my parents' voices was gone, replaced by strange, urgent voices, bright lights, and needles poking me every which way. Thankfully, fifteen days later, my parents could hold me. But the trauma had lasting effects.

The reality is, my fear of the danger still lurking in Ford's Theatre is just one example of how I've struggled to regain control, safety and predictability in my life.

Thirty years later, I can laugh at the story. How does that saying go? "Kids say the darndest things." The story is laughable, sure. It also illustrates how trauma can linger. Unknowns are tough for everyone, but especially for somebody already struggling with factors outside of their control. Fear urges us to avoid unknowns at all cost, because the outcome could hurt.

REFLECTIONS

Now it's time for you to apply this lesson to your own life. Let's reflect and work on a few areas.

1. What good possibilities have you imagined or dreamt of?

2. What have you avoided out of fear?

3. What is at the root of that fear?

4. Recall a time when you moved forward in spite of fear.

Lesson 2

THE PROBLEM WITH
PLAYING IT SAFE

Working with youth and families affected by various disabilities, in my role as mentor and coach, has helped me realize an important truth. If you don't feel passionate about life, there's a good chance you feel like you haven't been given permission to dream and do. At the root is likely a form of fear. The greatest stumbling block you and I face is between our ears – it's in our minds. Past experiences, or well-meaning individuals have probably told us, "Play it safe," or "Better not get your hopes up," or "That's not for you."

Rarely have I been as excited as I was at the end of 2019. My wife and I were staying with friends when she spotted the travel deal of a lifetime. Suddenly, the dream I'd had to go to Italy since I was twelve years old was about to become a reality. She briefly asked if she should book the flights, but I was overwhelmed. I paced the room. This was my biggest dream ever, but I was afraid. I was afraid to hope for what I'd wanted so much.

What if my biggest dream didn't live up to my expectations? What if we spent considerable vacation time and money and were disappointed? What would that say about my hopes and dreams going forward? I decided we had to do it, and when she booked our tickets, I was elated. Going to Italy was pretty much all I could think about in the days ahead. I researched for hours and couldn't stop talking about it . . . Then news of the coronavirus rocked the world. So much for our trip, right?

Wrong! In the past, I would have said, "I knew I shouldn't have gotten my hopes up!" I would have been filled with doubt. I would have retreated back to the safety of low expectations.

Thankfully, I've come a long way from those negative thought patterns. Of course, my wife and I were disappointed when we learned the flight was canceled. We were also determined not to give up on our dream. We chose to renew our passports and take care of whatever details we could in preparation for our future trip. Now it's not a question of if, but when the trip will happen. As soon as we get the chance, we're ready to say, "Italy, here we come!"

Booking our trip to Italy reminded me of what it was like to feel fully alive through a desire realized. When you and I play it safe, we feel less alive—we forget what we're made of. We cease looking for opportunities and therefore don't recognize them when they appear.

When we are not fulfilled, we become bored. We settle,

we compromise, we waste. The alternative is to pay attention to what satisfies us and to pursue it. Don't give up! Let your actions match your higher vision rather than shrinking back. Squandering is a mark of unhappiness. Instead, invest and reap greater returns.

REFLECTIONS

Now it's time for you to apply this lesson to your own life. Let's reflect and work on a few areas.

1. Is there an area(s) where you feel like you don't have permission to dream? Why?

2. Have you paid attention to what satisfies? What have you done to pursue it?

3. Has playing it safe held you back from pursuing your dreams and goals?

4. Recall a time when you have been energized by stepping out courageously.

Lesson 3

ALMOST OUT OF THE QUESTION

As I neared the end of high school, I faced a tough choice about what to do next. I carefully considered whether to attend the University of Illinois at Urbana-Champaign. I knew I wanted to go to college. What I didn't know was whether I was ready or if I had what it took mentally, let alone physically.

For a kid who was once afraid of getting lost in the grocery store, due to disability-related perceptual problems, the thought of transitioning to a campus with more than 40,000 students was almost out of the question. Almost.

In the midst of trying to figure it out, someone I respected tried hard to save me from something he thought I would regret, namely being overwhelmed by a large university. "Maybe it would be wise for you to play small," he suggested. "Stay local. Do what you can handle. Familiarity will be around you. It'll be easier to transition." As the time to make a college decision neared, I became increasingly restless about the idea of attending a small, local school. Even though my head couldn't figure out how it would all come together, my heart longed to explore the unknown.

The older I get, the more this truth resonates with me: Your heart will take you places your head won't go. That is, if you allow your heart to do so.

Making the shift to a campus double the size of my hometown could have been too much if I allowed it to get the best of me, but I refused to let that happen. Instead, I found a way to make it work for me. I learned to focus on only what pertained to me.

In contrast to the fears that might have kept me close to home, the reality was that almost all my classes and activities occurred within a small radius. When circumstances suddenly overwhelmed me, I fell back on the support available to me from the fantastic disability services department. I utilized its transportation services and kept the lines of communication open with disability specialists on campus.

If you're reading this book, I suspect that you, like me, long to get the most out of life. I encourage you, once you see a goal, stay focused so that little can stop you.

As Martin Luther King Jr. said, "If you can't fly, then run, if you can't run, then walk, if you can't walk, then crawl, but whatever you do, you have to keep moving forward."

Find a way.

REFLECTIONS

Now it's time for you to apply this lesson to your own life. Have you locked in on a goal? You'll get the most out of this book, if you have a dream or goal in mind. Let's reflect and work on a few areas.

1. How has your heart influenced your goals?

2. How have you found a way to make a challenging situation work for you?

3. Can you recall a time when you experienced a contrast between your fears and reality? What did you learn from that experience?

Lesson 4

FEELING 10 FEET TALL

If you're in emotional pain due to disappointment over not attaining your dreams and goals, my heart goes out to you. I've been there.

Nonetheless, the more I've fought to move ahead and not give in to fear and limitations, the more I've realized that there's almost always something I can do. The only one who can ultimately limit me is me and what I believe. The same goes for you.

If we don't think we can, we won't even try, thereby confirming our fears via self-fulfilling prophecy.
Let me encourage you, you can do more than you think. And as you do more, your thoughts will expand. In other words, actions, no matter how small, will change your grid for what's possible.

Several years ago, I broke through my fear to do something my mind told me, "No way!" Think again, my will and actions said. I chose to pursue what I wanted rather than avoid what I feared.

I was at a rope-climbing course with a group of friends, and I wanted so much to be included. No matter whether I saw a way, I would make one, I determined, as I set out on the course, 35 feet in the air. Rarely had I worked so hard. It was truly mind over matter, but in the process, I defied what I thought was possible and achieved a new level of belief in myself.

Afterward, my peers celebrated my accomplishment, and I felt ten feet tall. That wouldn't have happened if I hadn't made up my mind to try. I realized that day, I make the final call on what's possible in my life. You do, too.

REFLECTIONS

Now it's time for you to apply this lesson to your own life. Let's reflect and work on a few areas.

1. Does the subject of dreams and goals cause you pain?

2. Is it time to try again, despite what your memories may tell you? If not, what do you need to be able to give it another go?

3. When was the last time you faced your fear(s) and broke through?

4. Where do you need to make "the final call of what's possible" in your life, like I described?

My semester studying in Costa Rica was one of the most profound experiences of my life, largely due to my host family. (L to R Rigoberto, me, Lorena and Mati)

PART TWO

BREAKING FREE

Deep inside, we either know what we are capable of or we long to find out. It takes courage to go after your burning desire, your dream that you can't shake.

Lesson 5

YOU CAN BE UNSTOPPABLE

Do you feel like you are up against some pretty big obstacles when it comes to pursuing your dreams? If so, you're not alone.

One huge key to overcoming these obstacles is letting what's inside of you – grit, will and determination grow to be bigger than what you're facing on the outside. I learned this early in life as a result of my cerebral palsy.

Mom recalls a hot summer day when I was about three years-old and still not walking. She was pushing me around the neighborhood in a stroller when, suddenly, I demanded to be lifted out. "I want to walk, I want to walk," I insisted.

Nevermind that the temperature was in the 90s. Again and again, I attempted to walk. Again and again, I hit the pavement and stood back up, refusing to surrender to what many considered an impossibility.

My mom, in her wisdom, knew a few falls wouldn't hurt

me long-term. This was the moment we'd been waiting for. To deny me this opportunity for breakthrough and independence would have been far more damaging than a few bumps and bruises.

I knew what I was capable of, and nothing could stop me. How about you? Deep inside, what do you know you can do?

Your breakthrough moment awaits on the other side of this discovery.

REFLECTIONS

Now it's time for you to apply this lesson to your own life. Let's reflect and work on a few areas.

1. Are you willing to risk a figurative fall, if it leads to growth?

2. Where have you gotten up from falling in your life? What has that produced in you?

3. Deep inside, what do you know you can do? Have you determined not to quit or be denied?

Lesson 6

"OUT OF YOUR MESS
COMES YOUR MESSAGE"

It may sound like wishful thinking or crazy talk, but I'm here to tell you from experience that your greatest challenges need not keep you from where you want to go or what you want to do.

Not only was my walking delayed, I also struggled to write. For those of you familiar with special education terms, my early childhood IEP (Individualized Education Plan) goal for three years was that I would learn to write an 'x' and a 't.' (All the other letters would have to wait!) A variety of professionals tried any number of approaches, but I couldn't get it perceptually. Giving up wasn't an option.

At long last, breakthrough came. Mom switched to a sensory approach, which helped to untangle disconnected nerves in my brain. She'd do things like trace on my back or have me trace sandpaper letters with my finger. That repeated input gave my brain what it needed.

Something connected.

Three years after my first attempt, I made pretty good x's and t's. You could say my budding writing ability offered a clue to my future, too. For twelve years, I fulfilled my dream to be a professional sports writer.

My career journey reminds me of one of my favorite sayings from a mentor of mine: "Out of your mess comes your message."

Your circumstances don't have to limit you. You, too, can find a way.

REFLECTIONS

Now it's time for you to apply this lesson to your own life. Let's reflect and work on a few areas.

1. Is there an area in your life where it seems like you've been stuck a long time?

2. What if you were one breakthrough idea away from changing your life forever? Would you try again?

3. Have you involved others in searching for a solution to your struggle, or are you trying to figure it out yourself? Who could you involve?

4. How can "out of your mess comes your message" apply to you?

Lesson 7

NO REGRETS

It takes courage to go after your burning desire, to pursue the dream you can't shake. Every time you attempt to move forward, you're putting your heart on the line, making yourself vulnerable to rejection or disappointment.

Remember, though, chances are your biggest dreams aren't just about you. They are meant to benefit any number of people —friends, family, your city?—Who knows the impact your burning desire could have? The greatest dreams impact far more people than just you. Sure, there will be difficulty, hardship, and maybe even pain, but that is part of the human condition. Life is a struggle. Wouldn't it be better to struggle in your purpose than to struggle aimlessly?

A core question I ask routinely is, "What would I regret more? Would I rather try and have something not go the way I hoped, or not try and always wonder?" For me, it's usually a game-changer when I make a choice through that lens.

Spending more than twelve years in sports media left me with few, if any, regrets. I always went for the opportunity, even if it meant relocating eight times in ten years. Pursuing my dreams has taken me from Illinois to Detroit, to Costa Rica, from the East Coast to the West Coast, and back to center again.

People often act surprised when I list the different places I've called home. I never thought it was a big deal. Whatever it takes, that's my motto.

REFLECTIONS

Now it's time for you to apply this lesson to your own life. Let's reflect and work on a few areas.

1. Going after your dream means regularly putting your heart on the line. When was the last time you did so?

2. How is your dream meant to impact others?

3. Are you struggling in your purpose or struggling aimlessly? How can you tell?

Lesson 8

LOST IN TRANSLATION

Two years after I spent a summer working in Detroit, I landed in Costa Rica for a study-abroad program.

You know the saying, "The hardest part is getting started"? That was definitely the case for me.

I can still recall the cold, pitch-black night when I flew out of Chicago before dawn, en route to a foreign land. Upon arrival at Juan Santamaría International Airport, I grabbed a cab to the hostel where I stayed until I moved in with my host family several days later.

My four-year Spanish student award was apparently lost in translation, at least for the time being. Nerves and tiredness got the best of me, as I could barely manage a few words to my driver. The cab driver, although courteous, spoke broken English. Communicating was a challenge, as were other reminders that I was a long way from home. At that time, there was no WhatsApp or other international calling services. When the day came for my host family to pick me up, I clung to the last semblance of familiarity, watching an English broadcast of ESPN at the hostel.

Barely speaking to my host mom on the short car ride to my new home, I retreated to my bedroom as quickly as I could. I was in shock for most of the first night. "What had I gotten myself into?" I wondered.

Fortunately, my host mom knew the way to a man's heart is through his stomach. The next morning, she fixed a delicious traditional meal of rice and beans, along with fresh fruit. The bait brought me out of my shell. I went on to have one of the greatest experiences of my life.

Most meaningful experiences aren't comfortable, and require consistent flexing of your courage muscles. The good news is, the more you flex, the stronger you'll get, no question!

REFLECTIONS

Now it's time for you to apply this lesson to your own life. Let's reflect and work on a few areas.

1. Can you recall a time when you had a hard time getting started, but later the situation turned out really well?

2. What positives could be on the other side of your fear(s)?

Lesson 9

PURA VIDA

Spending a semester in Costa Rica proved to be another example of how something wonderful often awaits opposite our greatest fears. Rarely have I been so terrified of the unknown. Thankfully, I hung in there, and my love for Costa Rica grew steadily.

There were many reasons for my fondness, most of all was my remarkable family, which was a perfect match for me. Disabilities are challenging to navigate in any number of ways, but my hosts were as prepared as could be. Patriarch Rigoberto suffered an unthinkable work accident 30 years prior to our introduction. Electricity shot through his arms, ultimately leaving him lucky to be alive but also without hands.

You would think he would be bitter, depressed, apathetic or any number of other negative descriptors. Instead, he chose to look upward and rely on his faith in God. Talk about making choices. Daily, he awakes, puts on his prosthetic arms and cheerfully greets everyone he meets. I will always treasure the morning walks he and I took together where he recalled his youth and shared his wisdom with me.

Meeting Rigo will forever be one of the great privileges of my life. I never thought I could enjoy sitting in a lawn chair talking for hours at a time, but that's exactly what he and I did regularly. We played with the cat and dog, looked at the stars and enjoyed what Costa Ricans call "pura vida."

If only you could experience "pura vida" - the native Costa Rican term for taking life in stride, going with the flow and relaxing with friends and family - It's an attitude that leads to less stress and more happiness, and one that we international students soon adopted. For the first time in too long I gave thanks. It was a welcome change to leave pressure far behind for a little while.

Push through your fears, but also cut yourself some slack and go with the flow sometimes—"Pura Vida."

REFLECTIONS

Now it's time for you to apply this lesson to your own life. Let's reflect and work on a few areas.

1. Where do you need to hang in there in the midst of fear and uncertainty?

2. Who is someone who has inspired you and why? How has your life changed as a result?

3. What can you be thankful for?

Lesson 10

IT GETS EASIER

If you're like me, answering adventure's call isn't easy, but it gets easier. While still in college, I e-mailed the application for an MLB.com internship just before it was due at midnight. I was exhausted and felt like I had nothing left after finals, but I figured I might as well try. Incredibly, I was selected.

I spent my first extended time away from home living in Detroit, covering the Tigers' season. I loved Detroit - the people, the food, the history, and the baseball season I got to cover.
It's customary for media personnel to gather in the manager's office before and after every game. About two weeks into my internship, I was still finding my comfort zone and was shy and reluctant to stand out.

One day I gathered with about ten reporters in Tigers manager Jim Leyland's office. Leyland was in the middle of a conversation with the group when he stopped. Perhaps it was his father's heart, or maybe it was merely curiosity, but suddenly, I became the topic of conversation, as he asked me about myself for the next few minutes.

While that conversation was a highlight that summer, it was far from the only time I found myself out of my comfort zone and left to find a way. One night a cab driver dropped me off at one in the morning on the west side of the city, rather than on the east side where I lived. He didn't know where he was, and I didn't either. The one thing I did know was that I didn't want to keep paying for an escalating meter. I asked him to stop the taxi, I paid my fare, and exited. Maybe it was foolish, but I wasn't worried. I took a moment to get oriented, then began the long walk home.

Rarely, if ever, do you have all the answers you think you need. That was absolutely true when I moved a stone's throw away from New York City a few years later. One day a dear friend called with an opportunity. "No guarantees what happens," he said, "but if you want, I'll get you started on a job."

Make it there and you can make it anywhere, the saying goes. But, could I make it in the city that never sleeps? It was a long way from familiar comforts, and nothing like this small-town kid had ever seen before, but it became home. It wasn't easy, but between making friends, seeing sights, and adjusting to the big city, I learned to thrive.

REFLECTIONS

Now it's time for you to apply this lesson to your own life. Let's reflect and work on a few areas.

1. Has waiting for answers prevented you from moving forward? How long have you been waiting?

2. Are you willing to take a risk on an opportunity with few guarantees? What do you need to resolve ahead of time so that you can be ready when your opportunity comes?

3. Will you answer adventure's call?

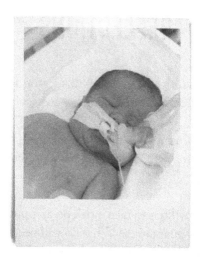

At birth, doctors did everything they could to keep me alive.

PART THREE

(INNER) HEALING

The topic of healing can be uncomfortable.
Coming to peace on the subject is crucial to
becoming your best self.

Lesson 11

WHAT DOES IT MEAN?

I'm not sure when I first realized I needed healing. Perhaps it was at age five when I suddenly sent out cataclysmic shockwaves by my matter-of-fact statement to my mom. "I have cerebral palsy," I said. It's doubtful I even knew what that meant. I did know one thing: it meant I was different.

Even then, my mom didn't want any limiting labels put on me and wondered who had told me. "What does that mean?" she asked. I proceeded to tell her my teacher had talked about disabilities in class and that led me to conclude that having a disability meant having difficulty walking, and as a result, wearing leg braces. "How do you feel about having CP?" my mom asked. "Fine," I responded. My response indicated that I was either in deep thought about the matter or that I was overwhelmed, shut down, and didn't want to deal with the thoughts and emotions.

Years passed before I consciously remember stopping to think about my reality. Stopping to think about my life could reveal even less control and say so over it than I previously acknowledged.

By the time middle school arrived, grade school friends, who had frequently stopped by my house to shoot hoops, play NERF bow and arrow or video games, visited friends in other neighborhoods instead. I felt left behind. They ran track and competed in sports there was no way I could participate in. For the first time, I felt keenly aware of what I could not do. I lost a student council election and faced the painful realization that I was not as popular as I thought.

However, even as I faced disappointment from people and activities I thought I could count on, I learned to rise to the occasion. I became the initiator with my friends. If I wanted to get together, I picked up the phone and called them.

As a result, I learned important lessons about valuing myself that I still refer to today. If someone won't readily call me back, it might say more about him or her than me. I'm so glad I learned sooner rather than later that friendships are two-sided and require give and take. If you put in effort, you deserve effort in return. You're worth it.

REFLECTIONS

Now it's time for you to apply this lesson to your own life. Let's reflect and work on a few areas.

1. Have you come to peace with your disability or how you are different? If so, what helped you get there? If not, what do you need?

2. Are you an initiator or do you wait for life to happen? What if you took more action?

Lesson 12

THE POWER OF LABELS

Perhaps, in one way or another, labels have told you that your power is limited and that your choices don't matter. Labels stick. Labels are powerful. Immediately after I emerged into the world, I was given a label: The doctor called me a "fighter" after I nearly died due to a lack of oxygen. I had no way of knowing the impact that label would have on me.

I've fought to prove myself for much of my life. I used to think that that mentality was a necessary part of life. Coping, struggle and isolation had become my lens. When you're fighting, you start to think that you don't need anyone, and that the world is against you. You shut people out.

That's why I'm so passionate about redeeming what was lost or stolen in my life, and in the lives of others. I now acknowledge the fighter mentality has advantages and disadvantages. It's good to be persistent. No question, tenacity is needed in life.

There's also the other side - thought patterns that fear the worst, that anticipate opposition. Labels like "fighter" inform our outlook on life. It's so important to process negative emotions in order to move forward. Process the pain and get professional help so that hope and freedom can emerge. When you do, it'll be much easier to follow the nudge in your heart that excites you.

REFLECTIONS

Now it's time for you to apply this lesson to your own life. Let's reflect and work on a few areas.

1. What are some labels that you or others have put on you?

2. How have labels affected you positively or negatively?

Lesson 13

CP DOESN'T DEFINE ME

Cerebral palsy used to feel like the elephant in the room for me. I tried to ignore it for fear it would crush me. I was told directly or indirectly by the culture that having CP or another disability meant having limitations, i.e. people with disabilities can't do that. I felt if I acknowledged my cerebral palsy, maybe what "they" said was true. Maybe there were things I couldn't do or shouldn't attempt.

Ignoring my disability now seems to lessen my authenticity. I realize I no longer have to fear acknowledging the fact that I have cerebral palsy. The higher truth is that it doesn't own me. I own it and tell it what I can do.

Typically I don't feel comfortable driving, unless it's for short distances on familiar routes. Instead I walk. A lot. For many years, I walked up to six miles a day, simply because I needed to get to where I needed to go. I recognize there is a wide range of cerebral palsy, and I'm grateful I can walk those distances.

While CP presents various challenges, it's also helped me hone mental toughness and resourcefulness. Those necessary walks (before ride-sharing became common) gave me time to do some of my best thinking about who I was becoming and what I wanted to do as a result. Coming to grips with who you are is vital to believing in yourself.

Sadly, a lot of the time we accept circumstances as "normal" or "the way it will always be." Suppressing pain is normal for many. If you feel stuck, the help of a counselor can bring breakthrough. That's why, when I started to sense my life was missing something, I went to counseling. Whoever says there's something shameful about getting help probably hasn't experienced freedom on the other side. When I found the help I needed, I experienced freedom I never knew was possible.

Make no mistake, cerebral palsy does not define me.

REFLECTIONS

Now it's time for you to apply this lesson to your own life. Let's reflect and work on a few areas.

1. Are you ignoring pain or discomfort? Why? What would happen if you owned it, like I described?

2. What is a positive, in spite of challenges you face?

3. Have you considered counseling? Why or why not?

Lesson 14

THANKS, COACH

Like a lot of kids, I was sure that playing for the middle school basketball team was my next step after grade school. From sun-up to sundown I was all about basketball—waking up to SportsCenter, reading sports biographies, and draining long-range threes in my driveway. I knew my basketball skills were unconventional, due to cerebral palsy limiting the use of my left side, but oh well, I thought. I'll just become the best right-sided player around!

As it turns out, basketball would play a part in my future, but not in the way I imagined. One-handed dribbling wasn't going to work. Instead, I became my school's announcing mainstay. If you came to a sporting event, the chances were good you'd hear my voice booming from the mic. After my disappointment of not making the basketball team, opportunities to announce became life-saving. I don't know what I would have done if I couldn't put my stamp on what I loved most. Being involved in athletics was central to who I was. In addition to sports-announcing, speech team was a huge part of my discovery process.

You might be able to guess, with my interest in sports, I am quite competitive. When I wasn't winning high school speech contests, I wracked my brain for break-through strategies in preparation for the next competition. It was my high school speech team coach who had an idea that would soon change my life.

She suggested I perform a monologue on what it's like to have cerebral palsy. Written by Facts of Life actress, Geri Jewell, who herself has CP, it's designed to be humorous and self-deprecating. Sure, I thought, If it could help me improve my results, I'm all-in. The more I practiced, the more I put myself into the piece. Audience reactions demonstrated I wasn't alone in my struggles, misunderstandings or pain. Reciting the monologue proved to be hugely healing for me.

My recitations resuscitated a part of me I'd apparently deadened from shame and a whole host of negative emotions. Slowly, I started to come to grips with my cerebral palsy. About that time, after five orthopedic surgeries, I was then given the option to have surgery on my problematic left hand. For the first time in my life, the decision whether or not to have surgery was mine. When doctors told me the procedure would only help how my hand looked and not its function, I knew the answer. Yes, I clench my left hand into a ball involuntarily and pull it to my chest when I'm nervous or struggling with a task. But why should I worry what others think?

I opted not to have the surgery. "Nobody's perfect," I reasoned. Some imperfections are a little more evident than others, and that's OK.

REFLECTIONS

Now it's time for you to apply this lesson to your own life. Let's reflect and work on a few areas.

1. Are you involved with what is central to who you are? If not, how could you be involved?

2. Can you think of a time when an activity was significantly healing or affirming to you?

3. Who in your life has helped you overcome pain or insecurity?

Lesson 15

CLOSER THAN YOU THINK

A friend once offered this reality check: "You can only own what you're willing to admit to."

Allow me to elaborate. One of the first keys to moving forward and gaining victory over your circumstances is to be honest with yourself. That could look like talking it through with a friend or life coach, or journaling, for example.

It's OK to admit that you're not really loving life right now. Be real with where you're at. Don't just stuff feelings down and try to ignore them. Process your emotions. Then make a decision to move forward.

I remember when I decided I was tired of feeling rejected and inadequate for a romantic relationship. It took counseling to address some limiting beliefs and behaviors. When I started going to counseling, I felt inadequate to date. I felt I was broken and that the woman I desired deserved better than me. I had to take what I could get after more capable guys made their choice.

This scarcity mentality I'm describing could also extend to someone who calls you names but says he's your friend, so you keep him around.

With the help of counseling and deliberate choices to push through anxiety and put myself out there again, I recognized my value to a potential partner. I began to identify how my giftings could compliment potential partners. I also chose to learn and use each experience as a stepping stone. I went on a couple dates. It was definitely uncomfortable getting started. I overshared and realized I was too needy. But momentum and confidence were building.

Surprisingly, once I confronted my limiting beliefs and discovered the greater truth about my worth, it didn't take very long before I was starting to win in the area I feared most.

It's by getting rid of negative emotions that you're able to make room for the good things that come your way. I can tell you from experience that hope and joy are closer than you think.

REFLECTIONS

Now it's time for you to apply this lesson to your own life. Let's reflect and work on a few areas.

1. Have you been honest about the emotions you feel and the decisions you've made in your life?

2. If you're struggling in life right now, have you thought about how you could take steps forward?

3. Recall a time when you got rid of a negative emotion and that made room for a positive.

Lesson 16

COMMIT TO THE PROCESS

Like anything worthwhile, inner-healing might take time, repeated effort, and help from a professional, but I encourage you to commit to the process of becoming your best self. It's not easy or for the faint of heart, but it's one of the most transformative, rewarding pursuits you'll ever do, if you choose to engage.

I have to warn you, you might confront ugly truths you don't like about yourself. I sure have. I've confronted feelings of self-hatred, and thoughts like "no one understands me." Yet, if the emotional healing process is done correctly, the way out of pain and limitations becomes clearer and clearer the more work you put in. With professional help, I've become excited about the privilege of being me, as well as of helping others understand what makes me come alive and how I can benefit them.

When you come to a roadblock, finding the right professional can be life-changing. Of course, it's vital that you find the right fit so you can feel safe and move forward. Trust your inner witness. You're probably more aware of what's helpful and of your needs than you think.

I sought counseling because I knew I needed help getting unstuck. I was dissatisfied with life. Sometimes it felt dull and boring. Other times it felt harrowing and overwhelming. I knew I needed help getting over my fears and limitations.

I went to one counselor who suggested that I was overreacting and that I mainly needed to be patient. There was truth in what he said, but I knew I had idled for too long. I was ready to hit the gas. I came across multiple recommendations for a counselor who sounded like what I was looking for. I knew he would challenge me. I knew he would ask hard questions. Then it would be up to me whether or not to back down. I kept going and still go to him from time to time. At no time do any of us reach a point where we have it all together.

Don't quit on yourself or your self-discovery process. You're worth investing in.

REFLECTIONS

Now it's time for you to apply this lesson to your own life. Let's reflect and work on a few areas.

1. In what area(s) do you want inner-healing? What would it feel like to be healed?

2. Have you committed to the process of becoming your best self? How?

3. What are you learning about yourself through your process right now?

4. Do you know you're worth investing in to get the healing you need?

While studying abroad in Costa Rica, my buddy, Mike, and I took a cross-country trip where I learned one of my most valuable lessons.

PART FOUR

STOP SAYING YOU'RE SORRY

You are not a problem. You're worth much
more than you give yourself credit for.
It's time you start noticing it.

Lesson 17

YOU ARE NOT A PROBLEM

What if I told you that possibly one of the first things you learned in life is wrong? Or at least it could be.

It's a safe bet that, for most of us, one of our earliest life lessons was to say, "I'm sorry." The thing is, what if that went too far? In fact, I'm going to make a statement right here multiple times for emphasis.

You are not a problem. You are not a problem. You are not a problem.

You may be thinking, "Sam, I know that." But I wonder if you really do? And, let's take it a step further: What do your words or actions demonstrate about what you believe?

I learned this lesson during a life-changing semester in Costa Rica.

My friend and I were making the most of a spring break

trip across the country. He kept us moving at a fast pace, and, no doubt, I was worn out from the strenuous trip. It was challenging for me to navigate the bumpy trails and varied terrain.

While he went up and down with ease, I had to be aware of my footing every time I took a step. "Sorry," I kept saying, as I noticed him pausing for me again, and again. I don't know about you, but my weaknesses are especially evident when I'm tired. The good news is, there's opportunity in weakness, as I was about to discover.

My friend set the pace for our adventure, but he was also kind, observant, and generous throughout. Often he extended a helping hand. Noting my weariness, he encouraged us to take a break. "Sam," he said, when we had caught our breaths, "You say you're sorry way too much. What do you have to be sorry for?"

Good question, I thought. Maybe everything? As we talked, I realized how wrong I'd been, not only on that day, but for as long as I could remember.

I felt guilty for not being the best adventure buddy, for holding him back, leaning on him, and making him shoulder my weight. I learned through this experience that I had a tendency to take responsibility for what I thought I should have been able to handle, or what a "normal" person could. It was an attempt to compensate for my disability. Can you relate?

For years, I wrestled with what people thought of me.

In particular, I didn't want to be pitied, and that left me with one option. I had to be so uplifting and inspirational with my words and attitude that my positivity would eclipse any reason I had to feel bad about myself. I tend to be positive most of the time, so that approach worked for a while. Over time, though, I realized I created something that couldn't last.

Limiting myself to happy vibes only was unrealistic, unfair to me, and a huge burden. Furthermore, I realized that my persona didn't allow others to express their emotions around me. I've learned that it's best to be transparent, ask for help when we need it, and support each other.

My friend didn't see me as a burden or a problem that day in Costa Rica. Let me ask you this: Is it possible you expect others to see you as a burden, when the truth is, if you'd ask them, they'd see totally differently?

That day in Costa Rica my friend told me he was proud to be my friend. He wanted to take a trip with me, in spite of potential challenges or limitations. Yes, I did slow us down, but I also gave us more time to take in what we'd otherwise miss.

REFLECTIONS

Now it's time for you to apply this lesson to your own life. Let's reflect and work on a few areas.

1. What do you apologize for too much?

2. Do you know you are not a problem? How do your words or actions demonstrate that you do not see yourself as a problem?

3. How do others see you differently than you see yourself? (If you don't know, ask.)

I'MPOSSIBLE

Lesson 18

IT'S TIME

You are not a problem. Let that sink in. When I'm aware of my shortcomings, I find it helps to ask others what they see.

If what I'm suggesting here disturbs you, I'd encourage you to do what it takes to find out why. Many times people struggle to receive compliments or validation because of shame or unworthiness, for example. Does this sound familiar? If so, I'd recommend going to a counselor, until you can believe in yourself again.

There are times it takes action, like having a conversation or going to counseling, to overcome the pain of shame and feeling sorry for yourself. Don't stay in your head. Commit to moving forward, no matter what it takes. The old saying is true: You can overcome anything you put your mind to.

I remember the first time I couldn't stop feeling sorry for myself. I was around four years old. Attempting to blow-dry the hair on my Bert and Ernie dolls almost caused a fire. I didn't know any better, but after I realized the mistake I'd made, panic and shame gripped me. It's amazing how events like that can stick with you for years. That was the beginning of me feeling like whatever went wrong was all my fault.

Even though I made a mistake, I learned to stop dwelling on past failures.

Focus, instead, on moving forward.

As with all of the lessons I share with you, I'm still working on this one. It's OK if you are, too. It's a process.

Like it or not, people tend to treat you how you treat yourself. The more I've stopped apologizing unnecessarily, the more others have recognized what I have to be proud of. Regardless of your shortcomings or mistakes, you have plenty to be proud of, too. It's all about perspective.

You're worth much more than you give yourself credit for. It's time you start noticing it.

REFLECTIONS

Now it's time for you to apply this lesson to your own life. Let's reflect and work on a few areas.

1. Recall a time when you stopped feeling sorry for yourself and how good that felt.

2. How often do you see yourself as a positive instead of a negative in people's lives?

3. What do you need to give yourself credit for?

In my teens, I constantly sent letters for advice. I discovered that Bob Costas is truly one of the greats,
not only professionally but personally as well.

PART FIVE

FRIENDS & MENTORS

No matter how strong or capable we are, we
need others. Others need us too.

Lesson 19

BE LIKE GRANDMA

Surrounding myself with quality people has made a huge difference in my life. But how did I manage to be so blessed? Partly it's due to my Grandma's example. She lived her life by the saying, "If you want to have a friend, be a friend."

Over the course of twenty years, I attended many meals in the dining room of Grandma's retirement home. Every time we ate together, I noticed the same thing: Grandma knew everybody and everybody knew her. What's more, they were happy to see her. She had words of encouragement for each person.

Maybe one of the more unique qualities about me is that I love spending time with senior citizens. Both of my grandpas died when I was young. Still, I cling to memories of time spent with them, and with my grandmas, too. Since their passing, I've deliberately sought surrogate grandparents who I can love and receive love from.

We all need each other, old and young alike. I've found

younger people have passion but lack the wisdom of experience. Seniors have wisdom but often are run down by life. One of life's greatest tragedies is what we miss out on. Opportunities for multigenerational relationships go untapped, and loneliness and ignorance persist on account of disconnection between the generations.

Let me encourage you, you don't have to miss out! Next time you run into someone from a generation or two ahead of you, say hello and initiate a conversation. Chances are, the senior will be surprised. You might be too. There's no doubt, questions are best answered by experience. Be on the lookout for opportunities to inquire. The answers you receive may change your life.

REFLECTIONS

Now it's time for you to apply this lesson to your own life. Let's reflect and work on a few areas.

1. How have you developed your friendships? Have you taken the initiative, like Grandma did?

2. What are your views on senior citizens? Is there a senior you could reach out to and learn from?

Lesson 20

RELATIONSHIPS MAKE LIFE WORTHWHILE

Relationships are what make life worthwhile. Through them, I became who I am.

Who would have ever thought that a bus driver, a farmer, a hairdresser, a pastor and a Spanish teacher would all play significant roles in shaping who I am? But they have, and so have many others.

When it came time to leave the nest, so to speak, I found the "siblings" I always wanted in my fraternity at the University of Illinois. For the first time, I understood the value of community, the idea that we all need others to help us grow, and they need us too.

The week I joined my fraternity was harrowing for me, to say the least. Known as I-Week, ultimately nothing crazy happened. No crazy stories sworn to secrecy. But for a risk-averse kid, partly due to CP, the week was enough to spike anxiety.

Rumors swirled about the physical, mental and emotional challenges awaiting us. Who knew what could happen at any moment. Looking back, it sounds laughable, but at the time, it felt like everyone wielded power and control, except for me and my initiate brothers.

Ultimately, we all bonded through our shared experience. The week provided more proof that I had what it took, and that we needed each other.

Beyond that week, each member had different chores. It's hard for me to forget the time when I was cleaning the microwave and its glass turntable. Somehow my hand slipped and the turntable crashed on the floor into a million pieces. After a few moments of shock and embarrassment, my fraternity brother came to my rescue. I had made a huge mess. On account of cerebral palsy, sweeping is difficult and crawling on the floor, even harder. He saw my struggle and filled the gap, cleaning up my mess. I was thankful we had a strong relationship before my time of need.

When you go through hard times, you need others. No matter how strong or capable you are, you can't do it alone.

REFLECTIONS

Now it's time for you to apply this lesson to your own life. Let's reflect and work on a few areas.

1. Which relationships have shaped your life? How?

2. Do you have strong relationships that will help you through hard times? How are you building relationships now?

Lesson 21

THE BEST WEEK OF YOUR LIFE

I still remember the summer I went to camp. Its billing as "the best week of your life" was only a slight exaggeration. The camp had everything–fun activities, good food and beautiful girls. What more could a teenage boy want? It was only a week long, but I'm pretty sure my mom packed all of my worldly possessions. (You know, just in case.)

I started the week off feeling pretty good because I had known a lot of my group for more than a year. I figured they would be there if I needed help, and we'd make some fun memories. However, I soon realized there's a difference between hanging out at a weekly youth program in a controlled environment and going to camp.

My "big bro" figure at the time had good intentions, but he also had his mind on a girl. I was on the outside looking in, but I still needed help lugging everything but the kitchen sink. I hated to be a burden or to annoy him while his mind was elsewhere. Thankfully I learned a lot about making my needs known to my friends that week.

At the beginning of the week, I was counting on one guy to be there for me when I needed help carrying things, when I felt lonely, or for any need I might have. After all, he was the one assigned to help me and the one I knew the most. He had my trust, something I can be slow to give. Pretty soon, however, I realized that my needs were too much for him or for any one person to carry. I had to let other cabin mates in on my needs and insecurities.

Now, twenty years later, the night when I let others in still stands out to me. I had kept everything to myself and my one buddy until, one evening in the cabin, I opened a humongous package of Chips Ahoy! cookies. I didn't mean to be the center of attention, but suddenly all the guys were interested in what I had. It took a few moments, but I decided to share. For the rest of the week, the cookies served as a good-natured joke and as a reason to interact. By the end of the week, I didn't need the cookies. I discovered who I am is more than enough. I still talk to several of those guys today.

REFLECTIONS

Now it's time for you to apply this lesson to your own life. Let's reflect and work on a few areas.

1. Have you tried to do something by yourself when you should have asked for help? When do you need to speak up?

2. Do you have a need you are suppressing? How would it feel to share and have that need met?

Lesson 22

DON'T ASSUME

Around the time I turned twelve, I locked in on my career aspiration to be a sports journalist. How could I get there? Were there any shortcuts? What would make me stand out? I considered anyone who worked in my field of interest as fair game to contact. I wrote letter after letter to journalists I admired. Their responses illustrated a lesson that's guided me ever since—you never know who will say yes.

Don't assume you're insignificant and can't have the relationship, connection or important input you seek. Your idol, or whoever is significant to you, may not be out of reach.   If you don't ask, the answer automatically becomes no.

But, what if you ask?

You might wonder, "How can I find a mentor?" It's important to pinpoint what you need. There are professional organizations such as Toastmasters or SCORE specifically designed to help you flourish. Or simply reach out to someone you respect in your field of interest.

One of my first mentors came about in an unlikely way. My teachers knew all too well about my aspirations and passions. I was always talking about my dreams and goals. What I didn't know then was that my resource teacher, of all people, had the perfect connection for that point in my life. Her brother was an usher with the local minor league baseball team, and he was glad to introduce me to the team broadcaster. I was starstruck when the broadcaster invited me to join him for a couple innings in the broadcast booth. At that point, it was beyond my wildest dreams that someone I listened to every night on the radio during the baseball season would become my friend and mentor.

For several years via email, we discussed the ins-and-outs of broadcasting. Periodically, he'd critique me. As a result, I felt more and more like I found my place of belonging. His affirmations fueled my courage to take more steps professionally and reach out to journalists I would have otherwise written off as beyond my reach.

If you don't take action, thoughts tend to spiral and self-loathing kicks in. I've been there too often. A much better idea is to hunt for your "yes." Write letters. Connect on social media. Attend networking events. Progress, fulfillment, validation and joy are yours for the taking, but only you can seize your portion and change your life.

REFLECTIONS

Now it's time for you to apply this lesson to your own life. Let's reflect and work on a few areas.

1. Have you assumed a dream or goal is out of reach? Where do you need to try again?

2. In what area do you need a mentor?

3. Are you looking for your yes, your open doors, so that you can move forward?

Lesson 23

WILL YOU MENTOR ME?

I wouldn't be where I am without the guidance and encouragement of mentors. In my experience, mentors are individuals who have gone down the path I wish to go and are willing to offer me guidance.

There are several reasons why I've been so blessed by mentors. First, I sought quality people and was respectful of their time. Next, I did what they advised me to do. Having worked with several mentors, I can safely say, if you encounter resistance from a prospective mentor, it's probably because their previous pupils were slow to follow the advice given. Show you're invested by following up and helping them see what you've learned.

Let's say you put yourself out there and ask someone to mentor you, and he or she says "no." Remember that "no" doesn't necessarily mean "no" forever. It may be bad timing for the person you're reaching out to. Keep trying. Don't give up. The "yes" you're looking for awaits you.

Due to the nature of the world we live in, you'll probably

find yourself doing quite a bit of follow-up. I remember reaching out to a mentor for advice several times with no response. When we finally connected after two or three months of my attempts, the timing was perfect. He was in the middle of a course and wondered if I'd like to go through it with him. The feedback I received and confidence I gained made a huge difference.

It's important to note, some mentors are only for a season. Others speak only to specific areas of our lives. One particular friend of mine prefers not to be called "mentor." We have limited parameters, but the wisdom he has spoken into my life has been life-changing. The point is, no one should be considered an end all, be all.

REFLECTIONS

Now it's time for you to apply this lesson to your own life. Let's reflect and work on a few areas.

1. Do you have any mentors in your life? How have they helped you?

2. How good are you at follow-up when you don't receive a response?

3. Are you quick to follow advice from mentors?

Lesson 24

A FOUR-LETTER WORD

One of my most powerful life experiences happened in a community group that only lasted about a year, but each one of us was forever changed for the better. From the get-go, our leader established a culture of accountability and vulnerability.

We met regularly and encouraged one another to aim for our highest potential. Receiving positive affirmation from others as we each faced our own challenges set the stage for transformation like many had never experienced.

Remember, cerebral palsy impacted every area of my life, not just physically. The most painful and limiting constraints were in the mental and emotional areas. Wounds from daily falls were more than a reminder of physical flaws. Missing out on the life I wanted to lead affected me far more.

After only a few months of meeting with the group, I was astonished to hear myself say: "I love myself." I had no idea those words were inside of me until I said them. Still today, I marvel at my moment. That wouldn't have happened except in a caring community.

In that community group, I found my voice. I discovered I could impact my peers and make meaningful contributions in my world. Once I realized I was wanted, accepted, and valued, returning to isolation, which had so often framed the landscape of my life, was no longer possible.

I admit it. What I describe here is all together rare. However, it is possible to experience this type of community. Decide you want an experience like I described, believe it's possible, and don't stop until you find it. Inquire at your local chamber of commerce or library for suggestions.

Since that remarkable year, I've found a few other groups with similar dynamics, and here is what I know: Being a part of a community isn't as hard as you think. No one is without quirks, and you may be surprised by how much you have in common with others.

A leader in my life says this: Accountability is accounting for your ability. It's allowing someone or a group insight into your hopes, dreams and fears so that they can help you move forward. Accountability is far from the four-letter word that many of us make it out to be. That is, unless that word is "grow."

REFLECTIONS

Now it's time for you to apply this lesson to your own life. Let's reflect and work on a few areas.

1. Are you part of a group? How has it helped you?

2. Who do you know that would provide good accountability and spur your growth?

Lesson 25

CHANGE HAPPENS BY CHOICE

Stepping out into new opportunities requires courage and perseverance. You might be rejected. Life is challenging.

In the middle of a long job search, I questioned myself. "What happened to the 'most impressive sophomore' my school advisor had ever seen?" I wondered. Those days appeared long gone. It felt like my life stalled. The days and nights ran together. Nothing seemed to change or to matter, regardless of what I tried. Thankfully, one particular lesson served me powerfully: "Sam, it's OK to be down, you just can't stay there," a mentor told me. Ever so slowly, I started to see glimmers of hope.

If you look hard enough, there are almost always positives. You just have to be willing to go through the process, whatever it takes. It's not easy. Many times "process" sounds like a swear word, but the more I go through it, the more I recognize that what I am going through is about who I'm becoming more than it is about a goal or destination. Most importantly, what I'm going through will not be wasted, as long as I am open to learning from it. Allow the discomfort you feel to lead you into growth. Don't short change transformation by refusing to feel the negative outcomes of your experience.

During that season that never seemed to end, I found my most impactful mentor. I lost close to 40 pounds. I forgave friends who wounded me deeply. Healing happened.

A father figure once told me, sometimes you learn more in hard times than in good. When life's good, we tend to stay on autopilot. The truth is, change happens by choice. I chose to discipline myself to walk every night, whatever the weather might be. In the quiet of those walks, transformation occurred.

Trust the process. More is happening than you know.

REFLECTIONS

Now it's time for you to apply this lesson to your own life. Let's reflect and work on a few areas.

1. When was the last time you demonstrated courage?

2. Are you going through a process now? What is happening? Who are you becoming?

3. Are you allowing discomfort to lead you into growth?

4. What changes do you need to choose to make?

Lesson 26

WE'RE ALL CONNECTED

If you're like me, one of the last things you want is to be dependent on anyone. But after crisscrossing the US for work, I firmly believe we are set up to help others and others are set up to help us.

Who would have thought that a summer internship in Detroit would open the next door for me? Having grown up in the Motor City, my prospective boss at USA Basketball was keenly interested when he saw Detroit as my previous place of employment.

A couple of years later, what seemed like coincidence set me up again. I had made friends with a young lady during my studies in Costa Rica and periodically stayed in touch with her after our classes ended. It caught me by surprise when I found out she was living in California where I desired to travel next. I ended up visiting her and soon enrolled in leadership schooling nearby. While there, I met my wife.

I didn't plan any of it. I couldn't have lined it up if I

tried, but life has a way of unfolding. It reminds me of the game, Continuing Story. If you haven't played, you should! A group gathers and passes around sheets of paper, each person seeing only the line directly preceding. Each player adds one line with no idea of the broader story unfolding. The result is a memorable narrative, better than anything that could have been written independently. All of us play a part in each other's stories. If we pay attention, plenty of connection points pop up along the way. The question is, are you looking for them?

REFLECTIONS

Now it's time for you to apply this lesson to your own life. Let's reflect and work on a few areas.

1. Are you paying attention to how you can help others?

2. Have you seen in your own life how one connection or experience often leads to the next?

Kayla is what I need to a "t." We're thankful Lola, our
Boston Terrier, helped bring us together.

PART SIX

FINDING YOUR WORTH

Pursuing authentic relationships is the scariest
and most rewarding thing you will ever do
because it's coming from your heart.
You want people in your life who will help
you be your best.

Lesson 27

YOU CAN'T LIVE IN YOUR HEAD

Living in fear inside your head takes you nowhere you want to go. There is a better way.

Allow me to share a very personal and painful experience to illustrate the benefit of having conversations that lead to freedom.

My story starts out well. Kind of like a fairytale. I hadn't dated until my freshman year in college. I was blindsided in the best way possible – love. My roommate was tired of talking to a girl back home, so he introduced us. Both he and the young lady were and are great people. I unwittingly found myself in a love triangle largely of my own making.

Soon, she and I were exchanging countless texts, emails and instant messages daily – everything except what's most important. We'd never met in person. A lot of misunderstandings can happen like that.

Looking back, I missed all the signs. I refused to see them

or believe the truth. My two friends meant no wrong by me. They didn't do anything malicious. In fact, my former roommate drove nearly 10 hours to talk with me and move forward in an honorable way. He and this girl were starting to date.

My conversation with him should have been plenty to jolt me back to reality. Instead, I became more insistent and desperate. Eventually she'd come around and we'd live happily ever after, I convinced myself. The key word there is "myself." I involved no one else in the process because, deep down, I knew I was the third wheel.

That's why you can't live in your head. It's one of my main pieces of advice and will save you pain that took me years to heal. Invite community into your process. It's so important to invite people into your hopes, dreams and fears. The right people won't belittle you, or steal your hopes and dreams. Involving community as you reach for your dreams will strengthen you and increase the chances that what you deeply desire will happen in real life.

I didn't let people into my process because I was afraid, afraid that this "relationship" was my only chance. I was afraid to find out that I was inadequate.

Looking back, there is something else I should have done differently. Instead of convincing myself that something dead would come to life, I should have been open to other possibilities.

Years later, I met my wife, and I couldn't be more grateful.

You too, whether single or married, have what it takes to cultivate vibrant relationships, where others share in your process, and you in theirs.

REFLECTIONS

Now it's time for you to apply this lesson to your own life. Let's reflect and work on a few areas.

1. Are you spending more time thinking about what isn't instead of what could be? What would happen if you invested that energy on making positive changes?

2. In what area(s) do you need to invite feedback and community? In other words, saying to someone, "This is what I'm thinking. What do you think?" about a specific area you're working through.

Lesson 28

KEEP GOING

For years I sat on the sidelines of dating. Subconsciously I had bought into the idea that the woman I wanted was "out of my league." She was better off with someone who wasn't broken. As a result of this mindset, I became passive and powerless. Looking back, I now realize that it was easier for me to shut down than to face my feelings of inadequacy. Dating became high stakes, all or nothing. It took a long time before I found the courage to enter the dating world.

As I shared earlier, my first romantic pursuit nearly killed me. I gave it all I had and was rejected. Consequently, I had to fight off suicidal thoughts. So you know, it's not abnormal to have suicidal thoughts. Let's demystify this, right here. There's no reason to feel ashamed. You're not a failure if you've had these thoughts, but you do need to get out of the hole. Tell at least one person who cares about you about your struggle.

I love Abraham Lincoln's quote: "I'm a success today because I had a friend who believed in me, and I didn't have the heart to let him down." That's one of the main reasons I kept going and still keep going today.

At my lowest point, I reached out to a friend of mine. He's got more than a half-century on me and has known me for my whole life. All told, I knew he had plenty of perspective to draw upon, and I couldn't dig out of my funk alone. I needed help. We talked regularly, and his perspective helped validate my questions and struggles. He listened and helped me realize I wasn't flawed for having my feelings. He believed in me, and gradually I got over the hump.

Chances are, at least one person has invested in you. At one point, someone recognized potential in you and invested in you with time, affirmations or otherwise. They deserve a return on their investment. People you care about need your gifts and abilities. They need your questions and thoughts, your humor and wit. You have skills or attributes your world, the people you care about, need.

Much of the healing process happens when you turn from being inwardly focused on yourself and your problems to outwardly focused on benefiting others. For me, that often looks like calling others to hear what's on their hearts. I do so because I care about my friends and loved ones. As it turns out, by encouraging others, I am almost always encouraged too.

REFLECTIONS

Now it's time for you to apply this lesson to your own life. Let's reflect and work on a few areas.

1. Have you become passive? How can you "put yourself back in the game?"

2. What skills do you have that people you care about need? Are you steadily developing them?

3. Think of a time when helping others helped you. How did it impact you?

Lesson 29

SOMETIMES WE STUMBLE INTO IT

Each of us needs people in our lives who will help us be our best. That means people who will challenge us, help us grow, and at the same time, allow us to be free. Free to be ourselves, free from limitations and expectations, free from shame. Believe it or not, plenty of people with that mindset exist. Keep searching. Don't lose hope. My wife is someone who accepts and loves me for who I am instead of resenting who I am not. As a result of her love and support, my confidence has soared.

Pursuing authentic relationships is the scariest and most rewarding thing you will ever do. Why? Because authentic relationships require you to be vulnerable.

Nowhere is that truer than in pursuing your significant other. I often talk to people who want to be married but feel hopeless in their pursuit. They want to give up, but I reassure them that if they have the desire to be married, their heart has a reason why. Don't give up. Don't ignore the desire or stuff it.

The question is, how do you find someone worth pursuing?

Sometimes, we stumble into it. That was the case with the love of my life.

Kayla and I met while volunteering at a youth program. I remember when she walked into my life. She was loud and opinionated, with a bubbly personality. I'm typically reserved and down to business, but I was intrigued. Each week when I saw her, I looked for ways to keep the conversation going. Whether that meant taking an interest in her expertise in jewelry, or asking her advice about our students, I was no fool. I knew there was potential for a relationship, if I could find the courage to pursue her. More than five years later, I've found she's what I need to a "t."

Relationships take intentionality. They take courage, but the best relationships are well worth the work.

They require us to step outside of ourselves and be open to someone else speaking into our lives.

REFLECTIONS

Now it's time for you to apply this lesson to your own life. Let's reflect and work on a few areas.

1. Who helps you be the best version of yourself?

2. Can you think of someone who has challenged you, and, as a result, your confidence has soared?

3. Name one activity you are involved in or could do where you could develop meaningful relationships.

Lesson 30

THE TORTOISE
AND THE HARE

After I had my heart shattered a second time by another attempt at a relationship, it took decisive action on my part to put myself out there. Along the way, I had to decide I wanted love more than I feared hurt. Love and hurt are inseparable parts of this world, but a love like my wife, Kayla's, makes it worth it, as you'll discover with the love of your life.

Affectionately, we call ourselves the tortoise and the hare. Like the fable, it's been quite the race.

Fear is generally the driving force in speeding things up. You're worried you might lose out. Without hesitation, I'll tell you that slowing down and taking our time is the best decision we made. It allowed us to really get to know one another and why we are the way we are. It gave us clarity as far as what we were getting into, and affirmed the strength of our future together.

On the other hand, while it's good to take your time and

think things through, you'll never know everything. At some point, you need to trust yourself that you're making the right decision to move forward. In fact, there are some things you'll only learn after you commit because the relationship changes and grows.

It took about eight months before I came out of my tortoise shell. I decided at Chuck E. Cheese's - you read that right - it was time to make a move.

Remember, we met at a youth program. At the year-end party, I was still very unsure, but one thing I knew. Volunteering was our one connection. The school year was ending. If I wavered, who knows whether we would cross paths again. Decision time stared me in the face. I returned to my favorite question: What would I regret more, trying and being disappointed or not trying and never knowing what could have been? It's OK to think something through, all you analytical types. Just don't stop short in your head.

She and I said goodbye at the party. It would have been easy for me to think I lost my only chance. But thankfully, by then I realized, life isn't as all or nothing as we make it out to be. I hadn't swept her off her feet next to gigantic plush singers at Chuck E. Cheese's, but I had resolved to take action. I sent her a message when I got home.

Incredibly, she responded to my coffee invite with a yes. That was a surprise. I never expected her to say "yes." All

I knew was I had to keep trying and doing what I could.

Somehow coffee turned into a long walk together. Neither of us knew quite what to make of it. Was I too nice, she wondered? Was she too much for this sensible tortoise, I contemplated.

Either way, we had to find out. Never had I been around someone so fun. Thank goodness for her Boston Terrier, Lola. I'll forever owe that dog. Lola was my "in" for our second walk. Again, I was searching for ways to keep our momentum going. I noticed Lola frequently came up in conversation and used that to my advantage. "I have to meet Lola," I said toward the end of our first walk together. Besides that comment, I must have done something right. "I feel so much peace around you," Kayla said repeatedly as weeks passed.

We went on six "non-date dates," as we called them. I was scared to commit but knew I wanted more. Somehow she knew to not give up on yours truly. Of course, I knew I had to decide on my intentions for the relationship eventually. Intentionality is a huge part of who I am, as she came to know increasingly.

The week before her birthday, Kayla went on a business trip. It gave me time to think. I knew I couldn't stall much longer. I also knew I couldn't do without her.

By the time she returned, I had made up my mind without any idea how she would respond. I couldn't lose her, but it was still her choice whether to move forward. As she pulled up to my apartment, I asked her the biggest question of my life – yes, bigger than "Will you marry me?" – no way had that even crossed my mind. I just wanted my first girlfriend. "Would you be my girlfriend?" I asked.

No sooner did she say "yes" than I shot out of the car. In hindsight, I never expected her to say "yes." When she did, I didn't know what to do. Did it really happen? She must have said "yes." Otherwise, I don't think we'd be married now. Her recollection of my proudest and most embarrassing moment is similar.

Two years of dating and engagement followed. What got us started kept us going – we had fun and took our time. We also intentionally tried not to change one another. That's been one of our biggest successes and principles – you get to be you, and I get to be me.

Don't change for your love interest, and don't expect him or her to change for you. Part of the reason why Kayla has helped my confidence soar is due to keen perception on her part. She's good at spotting growth areas and how to encourage progress, but no one wants to feel like a project. We decided early on to be ourselves without changing to fit what we thought the other person wanted. We needed to have a good idea of what we were getting into long term.

Besides, suppressing who you are out of fear is exhausting and can only hold up for so long. Fear tends to grow irrational in silence. Addressing it can increase feelings of being heard and valued.

Now if you've read all this and are feeling skeptical about your chances, I have good news for you.

I believe that there are any number of possibilities. I struck out several times before landing the woman of my dreams. Keep trying and don't settle. Remember, what you see is largely what you'll get. Problems almost always have two sides, and fault doesn't lie with only one person. Make the effort to work through your issues. It's worth it. Nothing beats celebrating or crying together and knowing you are not alone.

REFLECTIONS

Now it's time for you to apply this lesson to your own life. Let's reflect and work on a few areas.

1. Have you settled for unhealthy relationships in your life instead of those that help you be your best?

2. Where have you changed to satisfy others instead of staying true to yourself?

3. Where is fear trying to push you into making unhealthy decisions? Where do you need to slow down?

4. Which choice would you regret more, trying and being disappointed, or not trying and never knowing what could have been?

Lesson 31

NOT I OR YOU, BUT US

Sometimes I feel bad asking for help. I hear the shoulds clamoring for my attention: "You should be able to do that;" "You should be growing in independence;" "You should stop bothering that person."

I know I shouldn't feel bad about asking my wife or a close friend or family member to help get my car out of the snow. After all, helping is what loved ones do. But I also know that loved ones have long days, and so, if there's any chance I should be able to do it, I feel bad.

At the same time, maybe someone else loathes doing the laundry or the dishes. I'll gladly do them.

Could it be that's how caring relationships work? By complementing each other?

My now-wife calmed my insecurities about this early on in our dating and left me wondering if she was too good to be true one night when we took a walk.
I still remember where we were on the night when I never felt more relieved. What began as an otherwise

humdrum night suddenly became 12 drummers drumming a million times over. Kayla told me the very thing that I never thought I'd hear from a date. She said she was "determined to see more than my disability."

Now that I've been with my wife for several years, I'm gradually realizing that "normal" is what we make it.

There are still times when my inability to do certain tasks results in a great deal of pain and frustration for me. I wish I could help my wife carry large objects, like recently-purchased furniture, into our house. I wish I could chop food more easily, and efficiently use a broom. But those are two-handed jobs, and cerebral palsy makes them difficult.

Over time, I've realized this about challenges: they can either defeat us or refine us. We all feel vulnerable and inadequate sometimes, but it is up to us to decide how we'll respond to those feelings. I've learned not to think less of myself for needing help from time to time.

Ultimately, we all need to be open to giving and receiving help and recognize that there are appropriate times for both actions.

REFLECTIONS

Now it's time for you to apply this lesson to your own life. Let's reflect and work on a few areas.

1. In which area(s) have you felt inferior? Have you ever let a challenge defeat you?

2. Who has been your greatest encourager?

3. Recall the last time you surprised yourself with a positive response to a challenging situation.

From the time I can remember, I looked for how I could make my mark on the sporting events I loved. Here I am behind the microphone with my No. 1 fan growing up, my Dad.

PART SEVEN

FINDING YOUR SWEET SPOT

You were born with skills pointing toward your destiny. Success hinges on your awareness and use of these skills.

Lesson 32

FOLLOW THE CLUES

Baseball has rarely seen a hitter as good as Teddy Ballgame. The Splendid Splinter, AKA Ted Williams, was the last Major Leaguer to finish the season with a batting average better than .400. As a ballplayer, one of his secrets was his patience, not to mention his unbelievable eyesight. Williams waited for pitches he liked best, and as a result, was successful hitting those pitches forty percent of the time. They were in his sweet spot.

You too have a sweet spot. You were born with skills and passion pointing toward your destiny. Similar to Williams, success hinges on selectivity and paying attention. If you're intentional, you can achieve the success and fulfillment you long for.

Clues to my career were evident at an early age. I loved sports and was good at speaking and writing. I remember winning Young Authors competitions. More significantly, I can still feel the charge I got from emceeing my sixth grade talent show. It was on that night I knew that I belonged behind a microphone. I used my personality and energy to keep the show moving. Parents and peers alike gave me compliment after compliment. I was naturally gifted, and I loved calling the action.

Around the time I started high school, public address (PA) announcing behind the microphone resonated with Chicago Bulls fans, due to Ray Clay's introductions of Michael Jordan and teammates. Inspired, I dedicated myself to announcing for my school's teams, developing phrases like "Trifecta time" and "Good as gold." Referring to my announcing skills, more than one coach told me, "You make your school the place to play!" Passion speaks volumes.

REFLECTIONS

Now it's time for you to apply this lesson to your own life. Let's reflect and work on a few areas.

1. What are some clues to your sweet spot? What skills and passion point toward your destiny?

2. In what areas have you been affirmed by others?

3. In what ways are you intentional about achieving success in your sweet spot?

Lesson 33

AT THE HEART OF IT

Often, favorite childhood activities that appear to have little long-term value actually have tremendous significance in our lives. Maybe a childhood interest in trading cards or lemonade stands will blossom into a knack for sales. The key, then, is to let the passion play out and to cultivate its development.

Fortunately, my mom regularly took me on adventures to open my mind up to possibilities. When I was six years old, she took me to the local newspaper offices. Newspaper staffers were surprised to see a kid touring their newsroom, but it planted the seeds for my future in sports journalism. I don't remember anyone ever saying that my passion was frivolous or stupid.

Some people complicate purpose and passion. Not necessary, I say. Childhood interests often pop up at an age when we are our truest selves before life tries to squelch our dreams. If you wanted to be a firefighter or teacher at age six, there was a reason. I'll tell you a secret. As long as you're on this planet, you still have time to live out your buried dream.

If you're reading this and thinking, "That's impossible," may I remind you of the words of Muhammad Ali: "Impossible is not a declaration. It's a dare. Impossible is potential."

I grew up with a borderline obsession with basketball. I loved watching it and reading about the game as much as I could. I also had a pretty good shot. My problem was I could only dribble with one hand, which meant my prospects for playing the game at a high level were limited. But I found a way to contribute and be involved, not just in basketball but in any number of sports. I began broadcasting and writing about them. Is it the same as playing basketball? No. Does it give me satisfaction and enjoyment? Yes.

Let me ask you, what is at the heart of that desire that's really important to you? For example, maybe it's not possible for you to be a doctor, a nurse, or a teacher, but what is? Something is always possible!

Let's take a deeper look. Perhaps at the heart of your desire to be a doctor, you love helping people find a solution to what's wrong. Or if you wanted to be a nurse, could it be that at the core, it gives you great fulfillment to help people recover from pain? There are any number of paths to your destiny. Don't let roadblocks or detours stop you. There's still time.

REFLECTIONS

Now it's time for you to apply this lesson to your own life. Let's reflect and work on a few areas.

1. Are you seeing through the lens of surviving or thriving? What's the difference from your perspective?

2. How did your childhood interests impact you?

3. Have you thought about multiple paths to your dream or goal? What other options might there be?

Lesson 34

BE TRUE TO YOURSELF

If you haven't already discovered it, living for others' expectations and approval can only last so long. The burden becomes too great to bear. Eventually, you have to own what you believe and why you live the way you do.

Transitioning from my sports journalism career into life coaching, motivational speaking and training is one of the hardest choices I have made. Sports was my world for a long, long time. I loved it. I thrived. Until I didn't. Gradually, I realized I was going through the motions. Others labeled me as Mr. Sports, so I had to justify their belief in me. Except it was no longer me. Not like the work I'm doing now. I was thinking too small for myself. For those who live and breathe sports like I did, it's a perfect path. Just don't be afraid to make a change. Resistance to change, rooted in fear, is often our biggest obstacle to sweet-spot hitting. Conversely, proving to yourself that you hold the power of choice is a huge win in itself.

Taking ownership and being true to yourself is the start of personal fulfillment. Over the years, I've come to realize that each of us is intended to have a sphere of influence. Each one of us has valuable insights and a message that needs to be heard. What's yours? What do you find yourself musing about over and over again? Chances are that's a clue to where you are meant to make an impact.

Pay attention to what catches your interest and respond affirmatively. A lot of times nudges seem pointless, but there is a reason for them, and if you listen long enough, you will understand their significance.

Will you pay attention to the voice inside of you —faint, hesitant perhaps—but oh so pure? It might be buried beneath logic and necessity, but it knows the way. Your heart knows the way to expansion and fulfillment. Will you let it lead?

REFLECTIONS

Now it's time for you to apply this lesson to your own life. Let's reflect and work on a few areas.

1. Are you pursuing goals to win others' approval?

2. What hard choices have you made or do you need to make with regard to your dreams and goals?

3. What is your heart saying? When was the last time you listened to your heart? What happened?

Lesson 35

SING YOUR OWN SONG

Can I get on a soapbox for a minute? Too often there's a scarcity mentality for people affected by disabilities, i.e. I have to accept my life as it is and take what I can get. I only have one chance to get it right. I know. I've been there. I still have to confront it, but again it comes back to this truth: "A disability doesn't define you, unless you let it." You were born to make a difference. There's something only you can do as well as you. Now I'm sounding like Dr. Seuss, haha!

Recently, I was at an event listening to live music. I thought I recognized one of the singers but I wasn't sure until she turned around and started singing a song she had written. "I knew that song was familiar!" I said. I just didn't know for sure until I put a face with the song.

Did you know each of us has our own unique life song? When people hear it, they know it's coming from you or me. Your song is yours through and through, and you have a special power over that song. It's like when someone covers an original song. It's not the same.

People know if the song is yours. That means we have to get away from striving to sound like someone else, to be someone we're not. The best songs are originals that seemingly come out of nowhere, yet if you listen carefully, the song is often a reflection of the singer's life.

Similarly, people who love to sing usually don't care what others think. They sing for themselves first. It might not be on key or performed perfectly. If someone likes it, that's a bonus. The main thing is they couldn't suppress the urge to belt it out any longer.

Discovering your life song is one of the most life-giving and rewarding activities you could ever do. Life is not meant to consist of waking up, working and going to bed on repeat. There is more.

REFLECTIONS

Now it's time for you to apply this lesson to your own life. Let's reflect and work on a few areas.

1. Have you had a scarcity mentality and been thinking too small? How could you think bigger and more abundantly?

2. Have you let a disability, which I define as anything that would seek to limit you from your fullest expression, define you? How could you re-define what's possible in your life?

Me and my grandpa. He died when I was seven years old, but it's surprising to see how many personality traits we shared. I am honored.

PART EIGHT

YOU GOTTA WANT IT

In pursuit of your dreams and goals, grit and determination are two of the most significant driving forces.

Lesson 36

I AM BATMAN

I've always been a big fan of Batman, aka Bruce Wayne. Of all the superheroes, I find Batman most relatable. Without super powers, he must simply use what he has to fight

Much of the time, he is well aware of his weaknesses and shortcomings. In the movie Batman Begins, the evil League of Shadows strikes a devastating blow to Wayne Manor and Bruce Wayne's family legacy. As he watches the bad guys burn his family home to the ground, Bruce Wayne is at a loss. He doesn't want to fight crime anymore. What's more, he's not sure if he's done anything of value. There's no way he can make sense of his emotions and loss on his own. It takes a faithful friend, Alfred Pennyworth, to help him regain perspective. "Why do we fall?" Alfred asks. "So we can learn to pick ourselves up."

If there's something I'm familiar with, it's falling. Until recent years, I used to fall over and over, sometimes multiple times daily. Every day, I'd face losing control of my footing and momentary panic as I wondered how I would land and what the damage would be, only to have to pick myself up again and repeat the cycle. My elbows, hands and knees sometimes didn't heal for months.

One of the more terrifying falls took place on a frigid winter night. I exited the city bus and cautiously walked in the direction of my apartment. Ice and snow approaching a foot deep covered the landscape, making it a minefield for yours truly.

I was a few hundred feet from my apartment when I fell. Falls only take a few seconds but seem much more like a slow-motion replay that leaves you at the mercy of whatever hand fate deals at the moment. Typically, when I fall, I take a few moments to regain control, catch my breath, assess the damage, think about how long it might take to heal, and then determine to get back up again. But this time, the circumstances were not the normal brush-myself-off-and-try-again variety. I could not stand on the ice, and there was no one in sight. Terror gripped me.

When I fell, my cell phone flew from my hand to who knew where. Frostbite, or worse, was a real possibility. In my panic, it didn't feel like I had time or strength to look for my phone. Who knew if it was even working after the fall. Even though my brain was convinced I had blocks of ice where my hands and legs should be, the parts of my upper body I could still feel took over. It was as if I were one large block of ice, rather than a series of body parts working together, but the snow and ice were solid and smooth. I used all the upper body strength I had left. I willed myself to safety, crawling the rest of the way to my doorstep and clutching the door handle with all the strength I could muster.

I made it because of my grit and determination. No one else could help me that night. Similarly, it's my conviction that dreams and goals are matters of life and death, not unlike what I just described. You're either stoking the fires of passion by taking steps toward your dreams, or, slowly, you are simmering down and settling for far less.

Too many people are miserable. They wake up and fill their day just trying to get by before they go to bed for a handful of hours, only to repeat the same cycle over and over again. The good news is, you have the power to start a new cycle that energizes you and gives you hope any time you choose.

REFLECTIONS

Now it's time for you to apply this lesson to your own life. Let's reflect and work on a few areas.

1. When you feel like giving up, who or what inspires you to keep going?

2. Can you think of a time when your grit and determination made all the difference?

3. What's a new cycle or habit you can start? When will you begin?

Lesson 37

OUT OF THE WINDOW

Nowadays I rarely fall. That's due to a combination of factors, but two of the most important are stretching and pushing my limits. Over the years, I've become grateful for people who stretch my capacity literally and figuratively. It wasn't always that way.

When I was five years old, my grandparents graciously volunteered to take me to physical therapy. Tactically defensive, I hated physical therapy and would often put up a stink. One day I smelled blood in the water, so to speak. Meanwhile, in the front seat, my grandparents believed the best about me and were blissfully unaware when I threw a wrench into the day's plans. Tossing my exercise shorts out the back window somewhere on Route 74, I decided there would be no therapy that day.

Almost daily, I spent countless hours stretching and doing physical therapy at home. My resourceful parents turned our downstairs into a home gym of sorts, long before home gyms became popular. We had a bolster swing to help me with balance, a barrel and any number of machines.

Academics challenged me through a different type of stretching. As I grew older, I spent three, four, five hours a night on homework, just to catch up with my peers. Eventually, Mom's tutoring and Dad's patience paid off. What I learned not only benefited my studies. It also strengthened my determination.

Over time, I came to realize that stretching is a good thing. Without it, we are stuck. In a literal sense, we forfeit flexibility. Figuratively, we miss out on opportunities.

Is there something you have been gifted with that you're also reluctant about developing? Let me encourage you, stretch yourself. You don't need to work out all your fears at once, but make progress. It's better to make steady progress and to recognize that you're on the right track than to get overwhelmed by what's required and give up.

REFLECTIONS

Now it's time for you to apply this lesson to your own life. Let's reflect and work on a few areas.

1. Do you feel stuck? If so, where do you need to stretch?

2. What opportunities could you have if you figuratively stretched?

3. When was the last time you stretched yourself?

Lesson 38

DEFINE GREAT

Many times I've felt frustrated, ashamed and misunderstood because I have a burning desire for greatness. But because I can't do what others can do, on account of cerebral palsy, some don't give me the chance to prove myself. Furthermore, I realize that my "great" effort may be considered less than great by someone with no apparent disability. That gnaws at me. Nevertheless, I'm learning to focus only on what I can control.

My "great" is different than someone else's, and that's OK. Ultimately, success is being the best Sam I can be. This requires cultivating self-awareness. Once we are used to paying attention, we can have a pretty good idea whether or not we have given our best effort.

Maybe I couldn't compete on the basketball court, but I could put my best foot forward in the classroom. I coveted the four-year Spanish award in high school as soon as I became aware of its existence. In Spanish class, I found what Sir Ken Robinson referred to as the "element." It is the place where your skill and passion come together.

Much was out of my control in life, but that award was up for grabs, and I knew it. Every day when I entered Spanish class, I flipped a switch. I was there to win the award. I didn't care whether others thought I was a teacher's pet. I knew what I wanted. It was validation, and it was a competition that I could win. Daily, I readied to pounce by raising my hand with the right answer. My teacher teased me, but he also loved my exuberance.

I've often thought of myself as an underdog. The truth is, I put in the work to win the award. Still, it was one of the greatest surprises of my life when the presenter called my name at the end-of-the-year banquet. I won the award! That was pivotal for me. Putting the work in with intentionality takes you a long way toward success.

REFLECTIONS

Now it's time for you to apply this lesson to your own life. Let's reflect and work on a few areas.

1. How do you define "great" for yourself?

2. Has there been a time when you felt denied the chance to prove yourself due to a disability?

3. Are you OK if your "great" is different from someone else's?

Lesson 39

PUSH, DON'T PUNISH

Push, don't punish. It's true that the only way to grow and to move forward is to push your limits. But think largely, from a big-picture perspective. There are days when we don't sleep well or we get bad news – any number of variables can impact our abilities on a given day and slow us down. That's OK. Just give what you have. Growing in self-awareness of your capabilities is important.

This whole book is intended to help you live powerfully, no matter your circumstances or the time it takes to accomplish your goals. "It's not what happens to you, but how you react to it that matters," Greek philosopher Epictetus said.

That's why my grandpa patiently refused to give up on his dream. He embodied George Eliot's quote: "It is never too late to be what you might have been."

From a young age, he worked as a newspaper boy. A few years later, he endured heavy labor shoveling coal in

Pittsburgh steel mills. For years, he worked as a factory manager to support his wife and three children. He did what he had to do to make ends meet.

Defying social norms, he lived out his dreams at an age when most people retire. He formed his own consulting company and traveled the world. Furthermore, he ran half marathons and cross-country skied in his 60s. When his knees gave out, he swam.

He was proof of what happens when you live from burning desire.

Given his legacy, is it any wonder that no matter how often I fell due to cerebral palsy, I got up off the pavement again and again? Your dreams and goals may take time and result in some bumps and bruises, but you've got what it takes. Don't be discouraged.

REFLECTIONS

Now it's time for you to apply this lesson to your own life. Let's reflect and work on a few areas.

1. Where do you need to push but not punish?

2. In what areas have you allowed delays and setbacks to limit your future? What actions could you take instead?

3. Do you put forth all the effort you have consistently, or do you struggle with an all-or-nothing mindset? What could you do differently?

Prayers helped me and friends through a hurricane and helped my friend, Gino's grandpa, Juan, live for almost a decade afterward.

PART NINE

ON THE JOURNEY

The subject of faith can be painful and
controversial. We must each go on our
own journey. I come back to my faith
in tough times.

Lesson 40

THE STRUGGLE IS REAL

I couldn't have made it without God. That was true on day one, and it's still true to this day. Everything pointed to me passing away on that first day of my life. Born premature, I was black and blue due to a lack of oxygen. The doctor didn't think I would make it. I was whisked away to a nearby hospital with a neonatal intensive care unit.

Mom, who had been receiving blood transfusions, was rushed by ambulance to say goodbye to her baby. Clearly, my birth was traumatic. Years later, my parents and I discovered that my peers' parents were praying for me during those critical days.

It's humbling to think that I am a visible reminder of answered prayers. Sometimes I struggle with it. I feel guilty for ever doubting God today. One miracle like that should be enough to last a lifetime, but those answered prayers were my parents' and their peers', not mine.

I've had a lot of struggles, not just physically but with

my faith. Many of those struggles are related to cerebral palsy and its effects. How could a good God allow that? I don't know.

What I do know is that I could be in a lot worse shape. I could be without the skills, talents and relationships I have. I have a lot to be thankful for.

REFLECTIONS

Now it's time for you to apply this lesson to your own life. Let's reflect and work on a few areas.

1.   Has prayer impacted your life? How?

2.   What do you have to be thankful for?

Lesson 41

PRAYERS GOT ME THROUGH

We're all human. Cerebral palsy makes me all too aware of that, along with my need for others. I come back to my faith in tough times.

You might ask, "What about your disappointments? Hasn't God let you down?" It feels that way at times, but something keeps me going.

All of us long for something bigger than ourselves to hope in. When life's not going as you planned, what do you return to? I've learned that leaning on myself can only take me so far.

The prayers of others got me through day one of my life. My own prayers helped me through school. Prayers also gave me the words I needed to heal and forgive amidst heartbreak. They helped me in a late-night cab adventure in Detroit, and later in a hurricane.

I won't soon forget Hurricane Sandy that took place while I was freelancing in New Jersey. My parents had seen a forecast and advised me to head upstate one fall weekend. Some locals agreed. So a few friends and I headed to my friend's cabin in upstate New York. The weather was beautiful there.

Little did we know it was truly the calm before the storm. Around nightfall, the winds and rain suddenly made themselves known. I barely slept. The cabin creaked and creaked and creaked. The darkness was palpable. Never had I prayed so hard in my life.

Sometime in the middle of the night, I heard my friend's grandpa struggling to breathe. I woke my friend, and a short time later we decided to call 911. Only one problem. Actually, there were several problems. It was pitch black, we were in the middle of nowhere, and the approaching hurricane was gaining strength.

Thankfully, God knew what was coming. Weeks before the trip, I broke my phone and got a replacement. Wouldn't you know, my new phone was the only one in our group with service. As a result, medical help arrived. My friend's grandpa overcame a blood infection and stayed healthy for close to a decade afterward.

God cares about you more than you think. He cares about the details.

REFLECTIONS

Now it's time for you to apply this lesson to your own life. Let's reflect and work on a few areas.

1. What keeps you going and your faith alive?

2. When life's not going as planned, what do you return to?

Lesson 42

QUESTIONS

God and prayer are the only way I know how to make sense of life. That's why, in the midst of soul-searching, I decided I wanted to experience a God who so many friends and loved ones talked about but I rarely experienced beyond rules and shortcomings. Searching has helped me realize that instructions, rules and tenets are usually there to protect and help us. We need order to make sense of this crazy thing called life. At least I do.

I still have lots of questions. You might, too. It's OK. God's OK with questions. Keep searching and be open to what you receive. Your heart knows the way. Find others whom you respect and allow them to help you on your faith journey. As you think deeply and intentionally each step of the way, you'll find answers to your longings. It might take awhile, but I'll tell you from my experience, it's worth it.

I understand the subject of faith can be painful and controversial. We must each go on our own journey. I rely on my faith in tough times because people I respect do the same, and I've discovered my faith centers me. What's more, curiosity is a big part of who I am. I often wonder why the Bible is the best-selling book in history. But while I wrestle with my faith, I've found enough that works that I don't try to fix what's not broken.

I'm not yet comfortable sharing my thoughts on God with others, especially with those who don't ask. This God stuff is a deeply personal choice. No one should be coerced into a belief system. But from what I've experienced, knowing God is about much more than a belief system. It's about a relationship. All of us want to be known, believed in and loved. All of us want to belong.

REFLECTIONS

Now it's time for you to apply this lesson to your own life. Let's reflect and work on a few areas.

1. How do you make sense of life?

2. Have you searched until you've found peace?

3. Is there someone in your life whose faith you respect? What can you learn from him or her? How can he or she help you?

Lesson 43

GIVE IT A TRY

For several years, I've been on a quest to get to the core of my faith –what do I believe and why?

As a result, I've never felt more alive and hopeful. I've never felt more like somebody cares about me. If you want to experience God like this —a sense that someone is backing you, a sense that someone believes in you and cares about what you care about —for me that someone is Jesus Christ. You can try other religions, but life with Jesus is not about religion. Life with Jesus is about relationship.

If you're interested, try talking to Jesus like you would your best friend. I'm not saying you will immediately feel that level of connection, but you might. What I am saying is the God I have experienced wants to have personal interaction. Tell him what you are excited about, what makes you sad, and so on. You might think he already knows that stuff because he's God. The thing is, he wants to be your friend, and friends usually don't pry without being invited.

Know too, Jesus can take the negative. He can take your venting or swearing, even if it's at him. However, just like when you are negative or swear at your best friend, you might need to apologize so the hurt doesn't remain between you and you can move forward in your relationship.

The point is, this God is bigger and better than you think. Tell him you want a relationship. What do you have to lose? It's the most worthwhile, authentic pursuit you'll ever engage in. No matter the quality of your other friendships, Jesus is the best friend you could ever have. Give him a try.

REFLECTIONS

Now it's time for you to apply this lesson to your own life. Let's reflect and work on a few areas.

1. What do you believe and why?

2. Will you go on your own faith journey?

3. Have you given God a try? Will you?

I spent summer 2006 working for the Detroit Tigers and MLB.com. It's no exaggeration to say my life changed forever, as a result.

PART TEN

YOUR DREAMS ARE POSSIBLE

Your dream is possible. You were created with your destiny in mind. With the encouragement of others and core values to return to in times of uncertainty, you can experience the life you long for.

Lesson 44

GET IN THE GAME

In my "Get in the Game" keynote speech, I reference longtime NBA player and champion basketball coach Steve Kerr to illustrate a need to hone skills and prepare for your moment. As a player, Kerr tirelessly practiced shooting. His preparation paid off when he caught a pass from Michael Jordan and knocked down the shot to win the NBA championship.

Kerr excelled in specialization. That's something we could all learn from these days. What's your area of potential expertise? Where can you make your mark? We're designed to impact our world. All it takes is steady application. You'll get your opportunity. It might not be on Steve Kerr's world championship stage as Michael Jordan's teammate, but your moment awaits. Will you be ready?

Discipline and preparation are essential to making what seems impossible possible. I'm talking about steadiness. You could be the best, a prodigy, but if you are not willing to develop yourself and stay current, you may end up like

Wally Pip. You're asking, 'Who's he?' Exactly. Instead, try your best to "Be Like Mike" – an overcomer. Remember, arguably the greatest basketball player of all-time was left off his high school basketball team. He wasn't good enough to make it initially. Fortunately for us, he didn't quit. He bounced back and found a way. Where do you need to try again?

Now let me say this. If you keep trying and getting resistance, it might be time to try another pursuit, to move on. Even Michael Jordan moved on from baseball.

It took a while for me to decide that a transition to speaking, coaching and training was best for me and the people I cared deeply about. Because any decision you make affects more than only you, I'd encourage you to involve others in your decision process, especially big ones, like careers. Just know, responsibility ultimately rests with you, and that's a good thing. You're more powerful than you think.

As hard as it was for me to transition from working in sports media, I've never felt more fulfilled. Working in personal development is what I was born to do. It's my purpose, where I can make an impact. Where can you make a difference? There are probably more clues in your life than you realize.

REFLECTIONS

Now it's time for you to apply this lesson to your own life. Let's reflect and work on a few areas.

1. What's your area of potential expertise? Where can you make your mark?

2. How disciplined and steady are you? How could you increase in those areas?

3. Have you considered trying another pursuit? What are some alternatives?

Lesson 45

TICKETS, PLEASE

*"For all sad words of tongue and pen,
the saddest are these, 'It might have been.'"*
— JOHN GREENLEAF WHITTIER, POET

I don't know whether to sigh, cry or get mad when I read that quote. I've experienced all of those emotions and more on my dream journey. And that's why I want to help you.

I remember when the idea of helping others pursue their longings and ambitions took root in my heart. It was on a day off in the midst of my internship with MLB.com in Detroit. Wearing my Tigers hat, I walked to the nearby Subway shop. The young man behind the counter spotted my hat and perked up as he made my sandwich. "Do you have tickets to the game tomorrow night?" he asked.

"I work there," I responded.

"Man, that's cool! I wish I could go!" he said.

Suddenly, in an otherwise ordinary moment, a seed was planted for a dream. Looking back, I realize that's how dreams often start. Like seeds, it's easy for them to go unnoticed. However, if we pay attention, seeds like the one planted in my heart that day in Detroit can bear fruit many times over. That day I determined I would offer young men and women, not unlike myself, tickets to their dreams, just as people have done for me.

Your dream is possible. Your best is enough because you are enough. But without the encouragement of others, we often find ourselves on the outside of the life we long for.

That brings me to the business of Dreaming Made Simple. Over and over again, I've seen the impact of accountability in my life. Coaches have asked me life-changing questions, based on feedback they received from me that showed evidence of ideas bubbling in me below the surface but unable to make their way to the surface without additional aid.

In my mind, few aspects of life are better than a client's "aha" moment. I've seen it time after time, whether it was coaching Chris through a process to minimize stress and maximize his time; training a class in SMART goals and how to focus on strengths rather than weaknesses; speaking to middle schoolers about how to take budding curiosity into a path that could lead to their first job and far beyond; or helping multiple clients find the clarity, courage and confidence to pursue their life partner and get the "yes" of a lifetime. I love coaching my clients through whatever challenge they face to the breakthrough they long for.

I'm Coach Sam. I coach, speak and train. I help you make what matters to you possible.

REFLECTIONS

On the following page, you will find The *I'MPOSSIBLE* Framework, a list of affirmation statements from each lesson in this book. These affirmations, reviewed and applied often, will encourage you and keep your momentum going. First, here are your reflection questions.

1. Have you had any life-changing moments? If so, what's different as a result?

2. What seeds for your dreams have been planted in you?

3. What can you do to help those seeds grow, and when will you do it?

THE I'MPOSSIBLE FRAMEWORK

I refuse to let fear tell me what I can and can't do. (Lesson 1)
I exercise courage to go after my dreams. (Lesson 2)
I develop my closest relationships with people who help me become my best self. (Lesson 3)
I am not a problem. I am set up to be a solution. (Lesson 4)
I will not ignore emotional pain. (Lesson 5)
I help others, and I am helped. (Lesson 6)
I am aware of my skills, and I look for opportunities to use them. (Lesson 7)
I put in the work to win. (Lesson 8)
I keep searching until I find peace. (Lesson 9)
I am confident my dreams are possible. (Lesson 10)

By applying the affirmation statements above, I was able to answer adventure's call, living and working in seven different cities in 10 years – each spot uniquely challenging and rewarding - They paved the way for me to work for Major League Baseball and USA Basketball. Most importantly, they helped me find the woman of my dreams and be the best husband I can be to her.

You may want to use these statements to springboard your own daily routine. Feel free to add affirmations that specifically resonate with you (You can start your list on the next page!)

Don't tell me you can't do something. "A journey of a thousand miles begins with a single step." Your best is ahead!

_____ **'S CORE VALUES**
(Your Name)

1.

2.

3.

4.

5.

Sam Miller is a life coach, trainer, speaker and founder of Dreaming Made Simple. He is dedicated to helping those affected by disabilities pursue their dreams and goals through encouragement and practical steps.

LET'S CONNECT!

I love helping people discover practical steps to reach their dreams! I also love learning and have interviewed the likes of John Maxwell, Arianna Huffington, Mark Cuban, and many other influencers for their advice on growing myself and others. I am a journalism graduate of the University of Illinois and have worked as a communications intern for USA Basketball, an associate reporter for MLB.com, and a freelance researcher for MLB Network.

More recently, I founded Dreaming Made Simple. Dreaming Made Simple offers coaching, speaking and training to motivated youth and families affected by disabilities so they can find a way to pursue their goals.

I am thankful to all those who are helping me to achieve my dreams and am eager to encourage you in your dreams. I believe each person has a significant story to tell and look forward to hearing yours!

Email me at sam@dreamingmadesimple.com. Or you can check out my website and Facebook page for more inspiration:

WWW.DREAMINGMADESIMPLE.COM
WWW.FACEBOOK.COM/DREAMINGMADESIMPLEPAGE

CPSIA information can be obtained
at www.ICGtesting.com
Printed in the USA
BVHW041217040422
633291BV00014B/741